WHY PUBLIC SCHOOLS?

Henry C. Clausen, 33°
Sovereign Grand Commander

THE SUPREME COUNCIL, 33°
ANCIENT AND ACCEPTED SCOTTISH RITE
OF FREEMASONRY
MOTHER JURISDICTION OF THE WORLD
1979

Library of Congress Catalog Card Number 79-66968.

DEDICATION

To all those public schoolteachers who see the noble vision of our children blooming into enlightened, loyal and moral citizens of the United States.

Sovereign Grand Commander

Front Cover: "The Guiding Influence," by Norman Rockwell, depicting the
guiding influence of George Washington on the Youth of America.
Published in the History of the George Washington Bicentennial, *Volume III.*

Back Cover: "The Little Red Schoolhouse."
Courtesy of H. Armstrong Roberts, Philadelphia, Pennsylvania.

AUTHOR'S OTHER BOOKS

Stanford's Judge Crothers, 1967
    Library of Congress Catalog Card Number 67-17964

Clausen's Commentaries on Morals and Dogma
    First Edition 1974
    Second Edition 1976
    Library of Congress Catalog Card Number 74-81092

Masons Who Helped Shape Our Nation, 1976
    Library of Congress Catalog Card Number 76-15904

Messages for a Mission, 1977
    Library of Congress Catalog Card Number 77-78489

Authentics of Fundamental Law for Scottish Rite Freemasonry, 1979
    Library of Congress Catalog Card Number 78-66003

TABLE OF CONTENTS

Prologue

"HELP us in our utmost need." That cry for help in Longfellow's "Tales of a Wayside Inn," could come today from our public schools.

An acute need arises because revisionists seek to undermine public confidence in this traditional cornerstone of our American Republic. Complaints are multiple. They come from those who dislike the busing of public schoolchildren for forced integration. This results in a withdrawal of the middle or upper class patronage from the public school system. Others claim there has been a seeming lack of graduates who can read and write English or do arithmetic well. Also, reports coming out of the classrooms of misbehavior, vandalism, crime and immorality encourage objections. Godlessness is also asserted, but the courts have never prohibited education about religion, only inculcation of dogma, such as the enforced recitation of a State composed prayer. All this is aggravated when teachers clamor for higher salaries or special working conditions and benefits, without giving any assurance of a better quality of instruction or student results.

Some of the detractors challenge not only the public schools as such but any education at all. They are not interested in an enlightenment of the masses. They, probably, would have agreed with Virginia's Colonial Governor, Sir William Berkeley, who wrote in 1677 to his home government: "Thank God, there are no free schools or printing . . . . God keep us from both." Perhaps he would have admired Theodoric the Great (454-526), King of Ostrogotha, who made sending a child to school a crime punishable by death!

Our Supreme Court has been alert to the problem and warned us in the *Everson* case of 1947 that in this country "two great drives" are "constantly in motion." One is to force the public to pay for church schools and the other is to inject sectarian dogma into the public schools. Of the total number of American students, 10 percent attend private and church elementary and secondary schools. More than 75 percent of these are enrolled in Roman Catholic church schools. Pressures for State funds and criticism of public schools therefore primarily come from those political blocs. The drive for funds takes various forms and disguises, such as the current clamor for a voucher system. The wit of man, however, cannot devise any scheme for such aid that would not violate the church-state separation intent of the Framers of our Constitution. A sequence of Supreme Court decisions gives strong support for this position.

From a policy standpoint, the current critics fail to perceive the role of a public school in the creation of social cohesion, or an American melting pot, whereby we produce a unified, enlightened and free citizenry. The essential nature of our nationwide public schools contributes better to a united community than the fragmentation of our children into many schools of diverse sects, special interests or competitive groups. That kind of segregation must lead to disjointed vagaries, with parochial or racial overtones, instead of an American speaking with one clear voice. At the same time, through local control of public schools and their individualistic approach, a citizen is pro-

Samuel Lewis
Courtesy of the
Department of
Education,
Columbus, Ohio.

duced who is not a cog in a State machine but a fully developed and free person.

Those who talk of "desirable" competition from private and church schools fail to see this would be cutthroat in character and, in any event, a grievous mistake. For, it would freeze the American boys and girls into widely divergent streams instead of into the cohesive confluence that only public schools can supply. As early as 1836, Samuel Lewis, first Superintendent of the Common Schools in Ohio, wrote these perceptive remarks:

"Take fifty lads in a neighborhood, including rich and poor—send them in childhood to the same school—let them join in the same sports, read and spell in the same classes, until their different circumstances fix their business for life: some go to the field, some to the mechanic's shop, some to merchandise: one becomes eminent at the bar, another in the pulpit: some become wealthy; the majority live on with a mere competency —a few are reduced to beggary! But let the most eloquent orator, that ever mounted a western stump, attempt to prejudice the minds of one part against the other—and so far from succeeding, the poorest of the whole would consider himself insulted."

If we delve into the history of countries other than our own, we confirm the wisdom and far-reaching beneficial results of public schools. Frederick the Great was a brilliant general and wanted to make his country of Prussia important in Europe. Before that, it was small and not very significant. He treated his people well and started a system of public schools for universal education. He waged war and added to his kingdom. Finally, his little country became one of the most powerful in Europe. When the nephew of Napoleon became Emperor of France, he wanted to be like his uncle the great Napoleon. So he created a powerful army, made himself Emperor and called himself Napoleon III. He was jealous of the neighboring country of Prussia of which William I then was king and who had a very able and extraordinary Prime Minister, Bismarck. In 1870, the countries went to war. Napoleon soon found he had made a bad mistake. Prussia completely beat Napoleon III, and he and his large army had to surrender. Then, in disgrace, he went to live in England. The Prussians marched into Paris and made the French agree to pay them five billion francs. As a result of this Franco-Prussian War, William of Prussia united the little German states and made himself Emperor of all Germany.

Remember the child. Pour out light and truth as God pours sunshine and rain. No longer seek knowledge as the luxury of a few, but dispense it amongst all as the bread of life. Summon the mightiest intellects: collect whatever talent or erudition or eloquence or authority the broad land can supply, and Go Forth and Teach this people.

Horace Mann

Later, the French leaders prepared a critique of why Prussia was able to win the war. Two basic conclusions were reached. First, Prussia was superior because it had the benefit of a system of public schools that Frederick the Great had started and in which all their children were trained and, second, because their soldiers were better drilled. So France set to work and started public schools everywhere in France. Since then France has been a republic, and the people have elected a president and an assembly.

A historical understanding of the public school movement in general and especially in America is therefore helpful. The aims and ideals and accomplishments, as well as the pros and cons, should be considered in proper perspective. The evidence thus adduced controls conclusions without singing any paeons of praise. The only possible objective judgment that can be reached after such analysis is that, on balance, the public school ideology and purpose are unassailable. Obviously, there is room for continual improvement of methodology. But rather than being monopolistic, the public schools have been an essential ingredient and the unifying force of America's freedom and greatness.

It follows that the drives of the revisionists should be stopped and reversed. They threaten the survival of public education, raid the public treasury for private purposes, perpetrate a cruel hoax because in all probability private and church schools would immediately raise tuitions, and knock down the protective barriers of our Constitution. Rather than hear the death rattle of a system that has served us so well for so long, we should summon back to awareness the reasons for its birth and dynamic career.

Looking toward the future we realize that we are headed

toward a new historical era in our technological world. As we contend or cooperate with other nations, we shall succeed or fail through brain rather than brawn. Unless our public schools are supported, protected and preserved, our Nation will be doomed. It is equally true that with a first-rate school system and its training of our youth for a free society we shall go forward and maintain our preeminent way of life. Hence, through our projects and programs for supporting public education, we help build a better America.

The hope of our future, clearly, lies in the education of our youth, with equal opportunities for all to study, learn and progress, each on his or her own merits in this complicated and changing world. This can best be done—indeed, it can only be done—in a system that provides for free public education.

There is yet another factor to be borne in mind. While in America we believe in the "work ethic," we still are imbued also with trust in what may be called the "worth ethic." Every little child in our country—and every other person as well—has a potential worth of great intrinsic value. What a glorious opportunity public schoolteachers have to inspire the hearts and develop the minds of their children, to help strengthen and assure a free Nation and society, and to serve as examples of truth and integrity. Yes, that is asking for school stability in a wobbly world, but this itself invites an exciting challenge.

The story of the public schoolteacher on playground duty shows how modern is the problem. She ran out to pick up a little boy who fell off a swing. He was all dirty and dusty, and as she tried to clean him she said, "Jimmie, please don't cry." He shouted, "Cry? I'm going to sue!"

It is my hope, therefore, that the institutional history set

forth in the following pages will merit approval of a movement that has been a series of triumphant victories for the
Nation and yet, at the same time, a central force in the
individual development of our children. Thus we shall
continue our advance toward an enlightened and unified
and free citizenry.

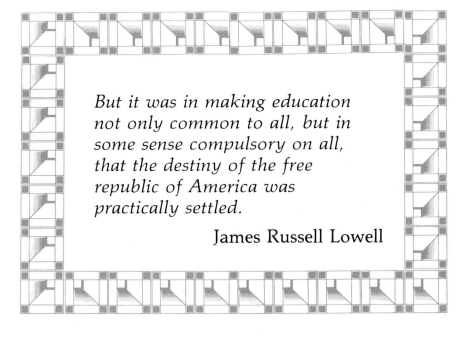

*But it was in making education
not only common to all, but in
some sense compulsory on all,
that the destiny of the free
republic of America was
practically settled.*

James Russell Lowell

THE AMERICAN
PUBLIC SCHOOL SYSTEM:
The Seventeenth
Century

WHY is the public school the cornerstone of the American Republic? What was its genesis? Why is it fundamentally and truly American?

We start in the 17th century. For free public education originated in colonial America. It developed through generation after generation, trained the diverse immigrants *to be* Americans, to revere *liberty* and to defend *freedom* at any cost. Of course, great citizens, as Benjamin Franklin, George Washington and Horace Mann, contributed significantly to the growth of American freedom. But under the shifting surface of economic, social and political change, it was the American free public school system that nurtured a freedom-loving people. To know this fact and to study its growth is to answer the question the French immigrant farmer of Orange County, New York, posed in 1782. He asked in his *Letters of an American Farmer:* "What is an American?" The answer is the story of the American public school.

The settlers of the first American Colonies came from England, Holland and Scotland. They brought with them Old World attitudes and forms of education. After all, the

1

Puritans were Englishmen despite their long stay in The Netherlands before setting sail for America. Therefore, they brought with them in 1620, as did the Jamestown adventurers in 1607, the attitudes of 17th century English society toward education.

England in the 17th century had no system of state-supported schools and had enacted no laws whatever on the subject of the literary education of the masses. Schooling of any advanced sort was the result of individual expense and usually was reserved for members of the upper classes of the gentry and clergy. Education of the general populace was managed only through the apprentice system. By the Statute of Artificers, all persons not engaged in husbandry or farming or of independent income were compelled to serve in either craft or merchant guilds. This system was an outgrowth of the late Middle Ages throughout Western Europe. The young man was apprenticed for a period of seven to ten years during which time he learned his craft and his master kept him. Once past his apprenticeship, he was a journeyman and worked for wages until he was admitted to the guild as a master workman.

Both in England and during their stay in The Netherlands, most of the middle class workers from England who settled in America's New England area were members of the weavers guild. They accepted the apprentice system, and transferred it intact to the New World. In Massachusetts, however, a very significant change in the apprenticeship laws was made. Apprenticeship in Europe traditionally had related only to training for a vocation. Literary learning was not taught except for minor exceptions related to skills necessary for commerce in the merchant guild.

The Massachusetts Colony in 1642 enacted a revolutionary alteration of the apprenticeship law because it forced the master worker to teach the apprentice more than just his craft. Under penalty of law, he also had to take care "especially of their ability to read and understand the principles of religion and the capital laws of the land." Here, then, was the germ of the American public school system. It was the first break in the wall of illiteracy that had confined the common man in the Old World. Note also that there is no mention of church control. The "principles" of religion were to be taught, not a religion. Also, there is a concern for education as a citizen in "the laws of the land."

The apprentice paid for his education with his labor, so this was not a "free" system nor was it "public" in that only young men, not women, were accepted for training. Yet, it began a trend toward the education of the average worker that continued from that time forward.

Only five years later, in 1647, Massachusetts passed America's first general school law. It provided that every township of 50 householders would "appoint one within their town to teach all such children as shall resort to him to write and to read, and whose wages shall be paid either by the parents or masters of such children, or by the inhabitants in general." A fine was prescribed for failure to comply.

Thus, for the first time in history, education became the responsibility of "the inhabitants in general." Up to this time, given the European flavor, free schools had been closely associated with poverty. The Poor Relief Law of England had imposed a tax for support of the poor. This was later applied to schools for children of the poor. Consequently, education and poor relief came to be asso-

3

ciated. Even under a charitable endowment, however, American "free" schools were few and generally were regarded as for students of "the poorer sort." Nevertheless, there were notable citizens such as Benjamin Syms, who in his will of 1634, provided a gift of 200 acres and a small herd of cows to found a tuition-free school for the children of Elizabeth City County, then part of Virginia.

Although the idea of a free, public-supported school system was established in Massachusetts during the 17th century, nevertheless, a tuition levy in the form of money, goods, or labor and church domination characterized the predominant forms of education, from the lowest to the highest.

Primary education throughout the Colonies began with the so-called dame school. Neighbors paid a local woman to teach boys the most basic lessons of the alphabet and

primer, and to instruct girls in domestic "huswifery" when attention to the primer lagged. The community members collectively had no responsibility for the dame school. The next step up the educational ladder was the "common" or writing school, similarly dependent upon the individual support of the affected families.

For students, boys especially, who needed such business skills such as "reckoning" and penmanship, a town school and schoolmaster would provide basic instruction. At age eight or nine, the children of the elite would enter a Latin grammar school to learn the *trivium* of Latin or Greek grammar, rhetoric and logic as a preparation for college. This school, the forerunner of the modern secondary school, was reserved for boys. A girl's education stopped at the dame school or her home if a private tutor could be employed. Typical of the attitude toward female education at the time, John Winthrop, Governor of the Massachusetts Bay Colony, advised girls not to attempt "such things as are proper for men, whose minds are stronger."

This Latin grammar school lead directly to college. There, as in every level of education, the influence of church authority was felt. Even when not actually part of a church, the ministers often taught schools and colleges in colonial America. They inculcated denominational dogmas more than classic knowledge. The English settlers, already accustomed to church schools in England, were of one mind with immigrants from Holland and Scotland in their devotion to the Bible. Martin Luther and later leaders such as Zwingli, Calvin and Knox of the Protestant Reformation stressed individual interpretation of the Holy Scriptures. How could this be possible and how could a man save his soul if he could not read?

The first objective of all education in colonial America,

therefore, was to learn to read the Bible so its teachings could be understood and followed. In addition, Calvinism stressed a close church-state unity that verged on theocracy in that the educated ministers naturally became the political leaders of their communities. The prevalent trends in colonial 17th century education in America stressed education under denominational influences or education as an expensive privilege reserved for the upper classes. Women were denied education beyond the elementary dame school unless private tutors were employed. The concept of a tax-supported, free public school system was generally associated with relief rolls, orphans and paupers. Yet, in this unpromising setting there were farsighted legislators, as in Massachusetts, who were beginning to recognize that for a people to be free, they must develop some form of general education which would be easily available to the masses and thus prepare them to be concerned, informed citizens.

The government and general court of Massachusetts had made the town school system obligatory for towns of 50 families or more. Towns of 100 households similarly were obliged under penalty of fine to support with a tax rate or individual contributions a Latin grammar school. New Hampshire, shortly after obtaining a separate legislature upon its separation from Massachusetts, in 1693, incorporated verbatim the Massachusetts compulsory school provision of 1647, and noted that "schoolhouses, and allowing a salary to a schoolmaster in each town" should be raised in "an equal rate and assessment upon the inhabitants." All citizens paid the tax; all students attended; control of staffing, course content and curriculum were in the hands of the secular authority, elected selectmen.

Here was the genesis of the first truly free public school system in America. It fixed the precedent for a free public school system. It was not an act of theory taken according to some preconceived idea of the proper role of education. In fact, the whole European heritage—whether from England, Holland or Scotland—dictated against the concept. The town records of these early communities reveal that the new plan of education originated in the people themselves. Through regular town meetings they sustained a direct interest in all aspects of local education, from the weighty matter of selecting a new schoolmaster to the replacement of a broken pane of glass.

The obstacles of prejudice, tradition and the very real difficulty of organizing schools in a widely scattered frontier society were overcome. When the 17th century was in its last decades, the burgeoning devotion to education and relief from the errors of the Old World can be seen in John Eliot's exclamation:

"Lord, for schools everywhere among us! That our schools may flourish! That every member of this assembly go home and procure a good school to be encouraged by the town where he lives! That before we die we may be so happy as to see a good school encouraged by every plantation of the country."

Without popular education no government which rests on popular action can long endure; the people must be schooled in the knowledge and if possible in the virtues upon which the maintenance and success of free institutions depend.

Woodrow Wilson

THE AMERICAN
PUBLIC SCHOOL SYSTEM:

The Eighteenth
Century — 1700-1775

FROM 1700 to 1775, there was a continuing growth in the general education of all Americans. The free public school system, developed from the 1647 Massachusetts compulsory education law had become a fixed feature in New England. This was an opportunity to surmount ignorance and stretch intellectual horizons. It spread throughout the Colonies, like waves from a rock thrown into water. In other sections of American, church affiliation and tuition payment remained standard aspects of education. There was, however, an increasing awareness of the advantages of the free public school system. Finally, the cultural revolution of the French and English Enlightenments, as it affected America, created a liberalization of the school curriculum, the decline of the old Latin grammar school and the rise of the more practical academy as Benjamin Franklin had outlined and created.

On the eve of the Revolution in 1775, the American people already had learned in the district schools of the New England Colonies and in the academies of the other Colonies the principles of individualism and integrity and, most of all, the value of freedom. They had thrown off, to a significant degree, the stifling and dogmatic control of church education. They were ready to face the challenge of a Revolution schooled in human values and dedicated to the defense of freedom. Significantly, the first actions of the Revolution took place in Lexington, Concord and Boston. The soldiers and patriots who fought these battles had learned in one-room schoolhouses and local town meetings their love of America and of liberty. They knew, as the great lesson of history, that slavish subservience will ever breed despotism and tyranny. The free public school system was an incubator, a laboratory that taught them the value of fireside Americanism and prepared them for the responsibilities of freedom. Verily, they became devoted Americans and accepted the resulting burdens.

Initially, in America, the school was the child of the church. Education beyond that given in the home was the responsibility of the clergy. This was clear in the original New England towns. Citizens were required to live within one-half mile of the town meetinghouse, to attend town meetings and to send their children to the town school.

At first, these meetings were held in the town church and ministers served as town officials, creating a type of religious republic. Financial support of education came through the church. At the close of the 17th century, however, the compact form of town settlement began to disintegrate as new settlements prospered on the fringes of the 20 to 40 square miles of the township. These pioneers, due to the dangers of Indian attacks and the difficulties of travel, especially in winter, began to demand their own churches and schools. Parishes were formed within the township. Then districts were created for the purpose of road repair. The isolated, independent settlements began to tax themselves to support a local school. Local citizens replaced the clergy as supervisors and schoolmasters. Citizens began to take a direct interest in the local school.

At first, to retain some control, the clergy of the central towns agreed to have a type of traveling minister-teacher move from district school to district school a number of weeks each year, proportionate to the amount of taxes for education that each district provided. Such centralization of control, however, did not satisfy the settlers. They soon demanded that tax revenues be returned to them for local administration in the parish or district, as it was called. In the latter part of the 18th century before the Revolution, however, local authorities were not clerical but secular, acting under the direction of the settlers themselves. They gained the right to elect school trustees, levy district taxes and select teachers. In the last quarter of the 18th century, therefore, the establishment of the district division and the resulting formation of a free public school system locally administered was well under way throughout New England. This district system in time would spread over nearly all the United States.

The simple record of this development is hardly heroic in a traditional sense. Though there were some great teachers, such as Cotton Mather, Jonathan Edwards and Ezikiel Cheever, the history of the evolution of the American free public school system during this first century and a half, from the earliest Jamestown settlement in 1607, to the Revolution, is not the record of the achievements of famous men. Rather, the system developed from thousands of acts of common laborers, farmers and businessmen. It was a democratic history, an undramatic harvest from the fertile soil and work of men and women at town meetings. Their names are not in textbooks or engraved on memorial plaques. Yet, these citizens were sufficiently concerned and courageous to do battle with the strongest institution of their time, the church, and to demand their right to control the education of their children.

This historic change ran counter to centuries of European development in which the church controlled almost all means of education. It also went against the very leaders, often Protestant ministers, who established the first colonial settlements. This was a great achievement in American history. School was separated from church, schoolmaster from minister or priest, tax from tithe, and education from religion. The separation allowed the child and future citizen to learn nondoctrinaire truth and to seek unfettered freedom. Only the broadest strokes of history can outline the heroes and events of this battle for freedom of a public school system. They fought the good fight for a good cause. The details of victory and of defeat, of who advocated and who opposed the concept of free education for all, are either lost or found in fragmented, uncoordinated form in the scattered town records of this early period. Yet, these farsighted pioneers, who were public school minded and who made their voices heard on platforms of the town, parish, district and state levels, are entitled to our deepest gratitude. Though individually unnamed, they should not remain unsung. The physical freedom of the early American frontier provided a heritage of spiritual and intellectual freedom that still benefits us today.

The economic frontier conditions which weakened the centralized town and promoted the rise of the district school also impelled these early Americans to local support and control. Similarly, a second ideological movement of freedom from fear was shaping the subject matter which was taught in the schools. The 18th century is often called the "Age of Enlightenment" in America as the new humanistic rationalism of the French and English Enlightenments came to America through the works of Voltaire, Rousseau, Locke and Newton. Diderot's *Encyclopedie* seemed to contain all knowledge. It expressed a faith in man's own ability and, while respecting the Deity, opposed spiritual despotism and political tyranny.

It has been noted that the Enlightenment affected America as deeply in the 18th century as the Renaissance had changed Italy in the 14th century. There was, in fact, a burgeoning in all aspects of science, art, literature and education throughout each of the Thirteen Colonies. For example, the Latin grammar school which had been in large part a training ground for gentlemen and clerics was forced to liberalize its curriculum and to lessen the stress on Latin and Greek and to add modern languages, sciences and mathematics. In fact, the elitist Latin grammar school, so often affiliated with a church or denominational college, yielded its place to a new educational institution after 1730, the academy. William Penn, in a letter addressed to his wife and children after his departure for America in 1682, clearly set forth the tone for the coming, more liberal 18th century in America. He said:

"For their learning be liberal. Spare no cost; for by such parsimony all is lost that is saved: but let it be useful knowledge, such as is consistent with truth and godliness, not cherishing a vain conversation or idle mind: for ingenuity mixed with industry is good for the body and mind too. I recommend the useful parts of mathematics, as building houses or ships, measuring, surveying, dialling, navigation; but agriculture is especially in my eye. Let my children be husbandmen and housewives. It is industrious, healthy, honest, and of good example, . . ."

The accent of the new academy was on practical studies. Closeness to nature and the frontier, for instance, encouraged the study of science, whereas, the rising middle-class capitalism of the seaboard caused a quasi-vocational stress on mathematics, accounting, geography, history and modern languages. America's population had grown from 200,000 in 1689, to over 2.5 million in 1775. Urban centers had expanded; trade with England and between the Colonies themselves had created a thriving commercial class that rejected the Old World doctrines of strict Calvinism for the New World optimistic faith in the possible moral perfection of man.

Preeminent among the leaders of the American Enlightenment was Benjamin Franklin. Never a recluse, pedant or narrow specialist, Franklin rose from his humble birth to become one of the greatest scientists, writers, humanitarians and diplomats of all time. Though educated at first in the apprentice system and then succeeding through his own efforts, Franklin recognized the need for a formal education that encompassed the whole man. In 1749, he expressed in his *Proposals Relating to the Education of Youth in Pensilvania,* a progressive, public-spirited view of the role that schools should play for the American people. The broad course he outlined included ancient languages, French, German, Spanish, English grammar, rhetoric and literature, history, natural science and other subjects designed to produce a practical, well-informed citizen. Franklin's proposed academy was opened in 1751, and, eventually, it became the University of Pennsylvania.

Clearly, Benjamin Franklin realized that a sound education was essential to the protection of freedom. In his *Proposals,* for instance, we find the following significant reference to the teaching of American history:

Benjamin Frank
Courtesy of the White House Histor
Association, Washington, D

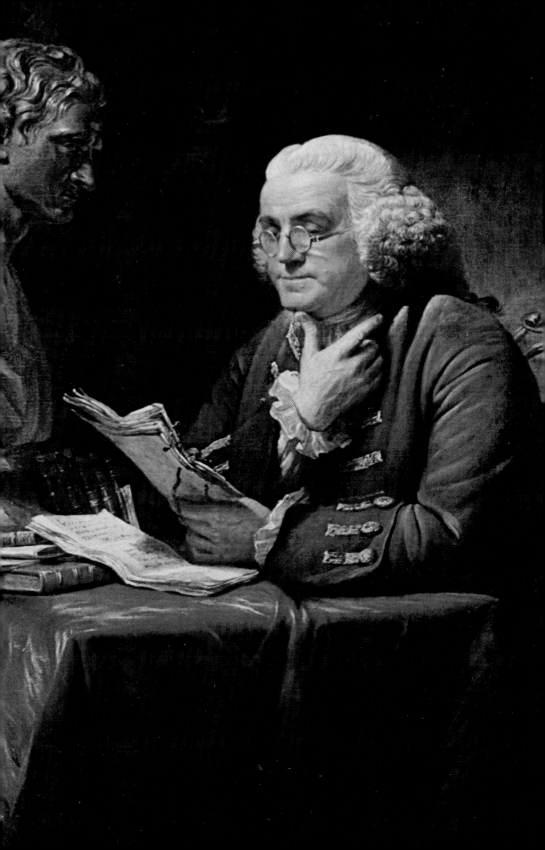

"If the new *Universal History* were also read, it would give a *connected* Idea of human Affairs, so far as it goes, which should be follow'd by the best modern Histories, particularly of our Mother Country; then of these Colonies; which should be accompanied with Observations on their Rise, Encrease, Use to Great-Britain, Encouragements, Discouragements, &c. the Means to make them flourish, secure their Liberties, &c."

Franklin's concept of freedom for the American people was based upon a firm foundation of public education. This was evident in his publication of the *Pennsylvania Gazette* (1729-1766) and *Poor Richard's Almanac* (1732-1757). Each aimed at educating the common man in both contemporary events and basic useful knowledge. Franklin sold over 10,000 *Almanacs* a year, and in 1755, there were 24 presses similar to Franklin's in ten of the Thirteen Colonies.

The good education of youth has been esteemed by wise men in all ages as the surest foundation of the happiness both of private families and of commonwealths.

Benjamin Franklin

THE AMERICAN
PUBLIC SCHOOL SYSTEM,
1775-1800:

"Education Shall Be Forever Encouraged"

THE American public school system, in a narrow sense, and education in general throughout the Colonies suffered greatly during the War of Independence. The last decades of the 18th century in America were filled with civil strife, military occupation, armed conflict and economic hardship. The American people turned their attention to the central question of the mere survival of the newly declared Nation. Freedom and independence took precedence over education. The armed camp replaced the schoolroom. America's budding local school systems, the newly founded colleges and the struggling academies tottered on the verge of collapse. Younger students were needed at home, in the store, and on the farm to fill adult roles while their fathers, brothers and elder male relatives joined State or Continental fighting forces.

It was in a purely material sense only that the American public school system suffered. For the American people had created in a spiritual sense another sort of school which taught nondogmatic lessons and truths. The defense of freedom motivated this more fully. The published

17

letters of the early Committees of Correspondence, the Declaration of Independence, the eloquent pamphlets such as *Common Sense* and *The Crisis* of Thomas Paine, *The Federalist Papers* of Alexander Hamilton, James Madison and John Jay, and the Constitution itself were a form of public school of greater scope and value than any that a local district could provide.

Teachers in this supernational school included the Founding Fathers themselves. Their eloquent words reminded Americans of the ancient Greek philosopher, Epictetus, who aptly said, "the educated only are free." And once the war was won and freedom assured, these great men reaffirmed their faith in a national commitment to public education. This was done in both words and deeds. In this national base the Founding Fathers fostered a growing general sentiment that acknowledged education for all as one of the essential functions of government and as a prerequisite for the preservation of a free Nation.

This was a new and farsighted policy. It evolved some three years before ratification of the Constitution. Under the Articles of Confederation an Ordinance for the Northwest Territory had been enacted in 1785. It called for a survey of the Ohio lands and directed that one square mile of land in each 36 square miles should be reserved for the support of public schools. This provision propelled further extensions as States entered the Union. More than 80 million acres of land thus were granted for the public school system. This was an area one-third larger than the combined New England States, and almost equivalent to the total area of Texas! No nation on the face of the earth, before or after that time, has been more generous in support of that purpose. The decision to provide a sound economic foundation for all later developments in American public education was truly epochal.

Two years later, in 1787, the same Congressional leaders adopted an Ordinance for the government of the territory lying northwest of Ohio. This provided that "religion, morality, and knowledge being necessary to good government and the happiness of mankind, schools and the means of education shall forever be encouraged" in the States to be formed of the territory. The force of these simple, yet enduring words, "education shall forever be encouraged," set the character of the American public school system for the entire Nation yet to be realized, from sea to sea. On its admittance in 1803, Ohio established this precedent for every State on admission to the Union, except Texas, which owned its own land when admitted, and West Virginia and Maine, which were carved from original States. In fact, after the admission of California in 1850, the grant was increased to two sections for each township and in the case of Utah, Arizona, Oklahoma (in part) and New Mexico to four per township, thus establishing an even broader base of support.

Other lands were added to these section grants. These are the present National Land Grants that form the basis for permanent school funds in all States west of the Alleghenies. In all, the national government has given these sections and other grants a total of approximately 132 million acres for public schools. This generous Federal policy greatly helped create a climate of friendly sentiment and persuaded older States similarly to put aside lands and moneys for their own State school systems. The development of this system was of great importance in an ideological as well as in a material sense because it encouraged States to found secular systems instead of copying the charitable, philanthropic or church systems of the older States in the East. It is no wonder, then, that Daniel Webster should speak of the famous Ordinance of 1787 as one of the greatest instruments of government ever issued. He said:

"I doubt whether any single law of any law-giver, ancient or modern, has produced more distinct, marked and lasting character than the Ordinance of 1787."

Thus, there was established a foundation for the public school system in the great Middle and Far West. The Ordinance of 1787 translated into reality the ideals of great men who, seeing the weaknesses of the Articles of Confederation, called for the convening of a Constitutional Convention that same year in Philadelphia. Franklin, Adams, Madison, Monroe, Jay, Jefferson and Washington were all firm supporters of public education. John Adams, for instance, expressed the feelings of these Founding Fathers as early as 1780, when, in arguing for a free public school provision in the Massachusetts Constitution, he said:

"The instruction of the people in every kind of knowledge that can be of use to them . . . as members of society and freemen, ought to be the care of the public . . . the education here intended is not merely that of the children of the rich and noble, but of every rank and class of people, down to the lowest and poorest. It is not too much to say that schools for the education of all should be placed at convenient distances and maintained at the public expense."

The Declaration of Independence in 1776, after all, had declared that "all men are created equal, that they were endowed by their Creator with certain unalienable Rights," and that "to secure these rights, Governments are instituted among Men, deriving their just powers from the consent of the governed, . . ." The fight for independence and freedom enforced the right of the American people to equality, freedom and justice. Logically, it would seem

John Adams
Courtesy of the White House Historical Association, Washington, D.C.

that education would be central to a Constitution and would assure the continued existence of its values. Yet, it was only implicit in the great document as ratified. But this does not mean that the Founding Fathers had not considered the issue. The records of the Constitutional Convention, for instance, reveal a discussion of the establishment of a national university at the seat of government. The fact is that the Signers of the Constitution realized wisely that rather than a nationally controlled public school system, the most desirable plan should be a local system under local control. Moreover, given the times and the scattered frontier population of the young Nation, a national system could not have been a success. Local townships, counties or districts had created and had control of local school systems, responsive to the people of each area.

This healthy and productive evolution was further sanctioned in 1791, with the ratification of the Tenth Amendment to the Constitution which provided that ". . . powers not delegated to the United States by the Constitution, nor prohibited by it to the States, are reserved to the States respectively, or to the people." The control of the schools and education, as one of the unmentioned powers thus reserved, thus officially passed to the people of the different States to handle in the manner they would know best. This decision was in keeping with the historical development of the American public school system as an institution the people had created and controlled. The intervention of a distant, central bureaucracy was thus wisely avoided and the public school system was kept in the hands of the people it directly served.

Secondly, Article I of "The Bill of Rights" attached to the Constitution, resolved another issue relating to the survival of the nonsectarian public school system. Article I asserted that "Congress shall make no law respecting an establishment of religion or prohibiting the free exercise thereof . . ." This action required the abandonment of State religions, religious tests, and public taxation for religion in the old States and to the prohibition of these in the new States as conditions for admission to the Union. It thereby constructed the firm foundations upon which our systems of free, common, public, tax-supported, nonsectarian schools have been built. It is impossible to conceive how we ever could have built a common public school system on a religious basis, with the numerous dogmatic and religious sects in our pluralistic society. The consequence would have been a series of feeble, jealous, antagonistic, contending church school systems, confined chiefly to elementary education, and each largely intent on indoctrinating its peculiar church dogmas and struggling and politicking for an increasing share of public funds.

Few have really appreciated how much we owe as a people to the Fathers of our Republic for this most intelligent provision. We trace to it not only the inestimable blessings of religious liberty, which we have so long enjoyed, but also the final establishment of our free public school system. It still required a half century of struggle with the churches to break their stranglehold and to create genuine public schools. This emancipation of education from church control had its genesis in this wise provision of our national Constitution.

Aside from their views as expressed in the Constitution itself, many of the Founding Fathers actively spoke and worked to foster greater public education for the emerging Nation. They tied the issue of education to freedom. For instance, James Madison, destined to be the fourth President of the United States, in corresponding with John Adams, wrote: "A popular Government, without popular

information, or the means of acquiring it, is but a Prologue to a Farce or a Tragedy; or, perhaps both." He held with Adams that liberty depended on the general diffusion of knowledge. "The best service that can be rendered to a country," he wrote, "next to that of giving it liberty, is in diffusing the mental improvement equally essential to the preservation and enjoyment of that blessing." Similarly, John Jay, the first Chief Justice of the United States, said;

"I consider knowledge to be the soul of a Republic, and as the weak and the wicked are generally in alliance, as much care should be taken to diminish the number of the former as of the latter. Education is the way to do this, and nothing should be left undone to afford all ranks of people the means of obtaining a proper degree of it at a cheap and easy rate."

Two great men stood out among the Founding Fathers in their defense of public education—Thomas Jefferson and George Washington. In 1779, Jefferson introduced a bill in the General Assembly of Virginia, providing for a State system of schools remarkably like the state school system of today. Then in 1787, writing from Paris where he had succeeded Franklin as American Minister to France, Jefferson advised James Madison to advocate education at the Constitutional Convention saying:

"Above all things, I hope the education of the common people will be attended to; convinced that on this good sense we may rely with the most security for the preservation of a due degree of liberty."

After his retirement from the office of President, "The Sage of Monticello," observed in 1816:

"If a nation expects to be ignorant and free, in a state of civilization, it expects what never was and never will be . . . . There is no safe deposit [for the functions of

James Madison   25

John Jay
Courtesy of the National Gallery of Art, Washington, D.C.

Thomas Jefferso
*Courtesy of the White House Historic
Association, Washington, D.C*

government], but the people themselves; nor can they be safe with them without information."

Jefferson's last years were devoted almost entirely to fostering education. He drew plans for the first buildings of the University of Virginia at Charlottesville and organized its curriculum. It was fitting that the epitaph he composed and which was placed on a simple obelisk that marks his grave at his beloved Monticello, reads:

"Here was buried Thomas Jefferson, Author of the Declaration of American Independence, of the Statute of Virginia for Religious Freedom and Father of the University of Virginia."

The idea that liberty cannot be preserved without the general education of all had no more fervent advocate among the Founding Fathers than George Washington. He applied enlightened concepts to the policy and practice of public education. In 1785, he established an elementary school in Alexandria, Virginia, and one of his greatest hopes was to establish a Federal university in Washington, D.C. As Chairman of the Constitutional Convention, he had ruled that a Federal Government could establish such a university to provide "the accumulation of the principles, opinions and manners of our countrymen by the common education of a portion of our youth from every quarter." To advance this project, the Father of Our Country, in 1795, offered to endow liberally such a national university in the Federal City. But the commissioners of the District of Columbia took no action. Also, in 1795, Washington wrote to the Governor of Virginia expressing his grief over "the youth of the United States migrating to foreign countries in order to acquire the higher branches of their erudition." He agreed to endow an institution within Virginia, and in 1796, he contributed a hundred shares of stock in James River Navigation Company to a little school called Liberty Hall Academy near Lexington in Rockbridge County, Virginia. That school is now Washington and Lee University, and since its donation the income from the stock donated by Washington has totaled well over $500,000.

Brother Washington's dedication to education for the American people was evident in both his first and last messages as President to Congress. In his first message, he advised: "There is nothing which can better deserve your patronage than the promotion of science and literature. Knowledge is in every country the surest basis of public happiness." Similarly, in his famous "Farewell Address" to the American people, Washington urged them:

> "Promote then as an object of primary importance, Institutions for the general diffusion of knowledge. In proportion as the structure of government gives force to public opinion, it is essential that public opinion should be enlightened."

Washington also again "proposed to the consideration of Congress the expediency of establishing a national university and also a military academy." No action was taken at that time, but Washington remained dedicated to his ideal of a national university. In his will, dated 1799, he inserted a long paragraph expressing his desire that the national government take action, and he bequeathed 50 shares of a Potomac Canal Company for this purpose. Not until 1821, did Washington's dream become a reality. President James Monroe and members of his Cabinet personally contributed to the founding of this institution, brought about an Act of Congress establishing the Columbian College, later renamed The George Washington University. At long last, the creation of a school of higher

learning in the Capital fulfilled, as President Monroe said, "the aspirations of Washington, Jefferson and Madison for the erection of a university at the seat of the Federal Government."

Like so many of the Founding Fathers, and even in the heat of the Revolution and the uncertain years of the new Republic, Washington was devoted to education as the means of preserving America and its ideal of freedom. True sons of the 18th Century Enlightenment, these heroic men understood Alexander Pope's observation in his *Moral Essay Epistle I:*

" 'Tis education forms the common mind: Just as the twig is bent the tree's inclined."

So to summarize: the vision of liberty and independence which inspired Washington and his patriot army to survive the suffering and despair of Valley Forge, could become a reality only through an educated American people, and a free, nonsectarian public school system was the best means of accomplishing that goal. It had developed from the earliest beginning of American history and had been proved practical in the New England district school system. The Ordinances of 1785 and 1787, established the principle of government support for education, setting aside township lands for educational purposes. The Constitution, through the Tenth Amendment and Article I of "The Bill of Rights," properly assured State and local control of education and guaranteed that the school systems would be free from sectarian religious influences.

Finally, in this period of the American public school system development, from 1775 to 1800, a series of great men such as Adams, Madison, Jay, Jefferson and, leading all, George Washington, demonstrated a far-reaching and fundamental faith in the American public school system as a unifying force of American freedom. The American people emerged from the last decades of the 18th century no longer colonials but as citizens of a united and ever-stronger Nation. They were, at last, Americans—free from political tyranny and spiritual despotism and in control of their destiny. They achieved this and proved their loyalty to the faith of their fathers through a public school system which embarked an idealistic people upon a heroic journey toward enlightened living.

The whole people must take upon themselves the education of the whole people and be willing to bear the expense of it.

John Adams

THE AMERICAN
PUBLIC SCHOOL SYSTEM,
1800-1850:

From Ideal Concept
to Practical Reality

As the year 1800 dawned, our Nation's greatest leaders had expressed the essential ideals of public education. The Ordinances of 1785 and 1787 had established the legal and economic basis in the States which would be carved out of the Northwest Territory. In the East, Vermont in 1782, Massachusetts and New Hampshire in 1789, enacted general laws to fund tax-supported schools. But as always there was a gap between the announced ideal and the accomplished reality.

Laws passed do not mean reforms achieved, for history moves in slow, steady steps, not in sudden leaps or turns. Our Founding Patriots, especially Thomas Jefferson and George Washington, eloquently had stated the indispensable tie between education and freedom. The Constitution wisely had delegated to the States local control of the schools, and the First Amendment clarified that public education should remain free of sectarian religious influence. Although the moral, legal and political foundation of the American system had been thus established, it would take another 50 years to make this a fully accepted reality.

Significantly, the American people, not the office-holders, demanded public schools. Citizens banded together in a number of voluntary societies to advance the idea. For example, the Pennsylvania Society for the Promotion of Public Schools was one of the earliest of such organizations. The American Institute of Instruction and The Western Literary Institute and College of Professional Teachers soon joined the movement. They published pamphlets, gave lectures and organized tours to advocate the cause.

Perhaps the most influential of these early citizen groups was the Public School Society of New York City. The chief organizer and first president was DeWitt Clinton, then mayor of New York City. He headed the list of founding subscribers in 1805, and promised $200 a year in support. Later, during nine years as Governor of New York State, he staunchly advocated the cause. In a message to the legislature in 1825, he defended the schools already established, saying:

"The first duty of government, and the surest evidence of good government, is the encouragement of education. A general diffusion of knowledge is a precursor and protector of republican institutions, and in it we must confide, as the conservative power that will watch over our liberties and guard them against fraud, intrigue, corruption, and violence. I consider the system of our common schools as the palladium of our freedom, for no reasonable apprehension can be entertained of its subversion as long as the great body of the people are enlightened by education."

Oldest Wooden Schoolhouse in the U.S., St. Augustine, Florida.
Courtesy of Beaudoin's Photography.

Late 19th Century Schoolhouse (circa).
Courtesy of the National Education Association, Washington, D.C.

Again in his message of 1827, he added:

"The great bulwark of republican government is the cultivation of education; for the right of suffrage cannot be exercised in a salutary manner without intelligence."

These societies and such perceptive and patriotic men as DeWitt Clinton gave great impetus to the movement. Economic and political developments helped their efforts. After the so-called "Second Revolution" of the War of 1812, American commerce and industry prospered. In 1800, only 4 percent of our population was urban. But in 1860, 16 percent of all Americans lived in cities. Urbanites and especially workingmen were eager to provide adequate free education for their children and so help them rise in the developing commercial society. In 1830, for example, the Workingman's Party of Philadelphia included as the first plank of its platform the following:

"*Resolved:* that the time has arrived when it becomes the paramount duty of every friend to the happiness and freedom of man to promote a system of education that shall embrace equally all the children of the state, of every rank and condition."

Similarly, in infant industrial towns such as New Castle, Delaware, associations of workers were appealing to new members with slogans that read:

"Let us unite at the polls and give our votes to no candidate who is not pledged to support a rational system of education to be paid for out of the public funds."

The rising prosperity of the cities extended to the pioneer patriots who, as veterans of the Revolutionary War, often had been given lands in the new territories. They realized the critical need for a State-supported educational system and responded to Daniel Webster's tribute to education in 1822:

DeWitt Clinton

Courtesy of the National Education Association, Washington, D.C.

". . . on the diffusion of education among the people rests the preservation and perpetuation of our free institutions."

It was not surprising that an ambitious young lawyer in Illinois, Abraham Lincoln, should campaign for office in 1832, saying:

"Upon the subject of education, not presuming to dictate any plan or system respecting it, I can say that I view it as the most important subject which we as a people can be engaged in."

It was in keeping with the spirit of the times that Ohio, upon admission as a State in 1803, prohibited pauper schools and in 1835 completed a State school system with certification of teachers. Whether in the city or on the frontier, the American citizen was willing to expend some of his increasing prosperity in the form of school taxes. His greater participation in politics was teaching him the value of an enlightened suffrage. The election of Andrew Jackson in 1828, saw the last vestiges of aristocratic control crumble and suffrage extended. Residence and property requirements to vote were either abolished outright or reduced to a rational minimum. It was realized that only literacy and education could provide a base for the wise use of the ballot box.

Aside from the economic and political developments that advanced the public school system during this transitional period from 1800 to 1850, there was the protective umbrella that the Constitutional provision of church-state separation provided. These decades show increasing release from church control and the ever-greater benefit of State support.

During these periods, however, immigration began to bring to American shores new religious groups and a

Abraham Linc
Courtesy of the White House Histor
Association, Washington, D

growing request for State monies to private church schools. But a firm stand was taken against this deviation from the intent of the Founding Fathers. This prevented any gradual encroachment upon state-church separation. In 1842, the Legislature of New York State took a clear, unequivocal position and stopped the controversy. It enacted legislation that provided no portion of State school funds was to be given to a school in which "any religious doctrine or tenet should be taught, inculcated or practiced." This significant proviso was incorporated in other State constitutions, usually upon a first vote. Every State admitted to the Union after 1858, except West Virginia, similarly so provided in their constitutions. West Virginia also took this step in 1872. It was realized that State support of private church schools would be a grievous raid of the public treasury, the death rattle of the public school system, and a violation of the separation principle that had been so wisely and firmly guaranteed in the Constitution.

These economic, political and legal developments formed the multiple foundations of the public school movement. One great educator in particular, Horace Mann, helped the system achieve success in the first half of the 19th century. He expanded and improved it in Massachusetts so it became a prototype for other States to follow throughout America. Horace Mann proved himself a hardworking, loyal and devoted friend of education. For ten years, in the lower and upper houses of the Massachusetts Legislature, and finally as president of the Massachusetts Senate, he backed bill after bill to organize and fund the developing State school system. He made eloquent addresses on this subject that revealed a statesmanlike determination to advance the cause. In 1837, he accepted the post of secretary of a newly created Massachusetts

Horace Mann
Courtesy of the National Education Association, Washington, D.C.

Board of Education. This, perhaps, was the greatest single event in the history of education in the Nation. He began his first year with total dedication to the duties of this office and wrote in his diary:

"Henceforth so long as I hold this office I devote myself to the supremest welfare of mankind on earth . . . . I have faith in the improvability of the race—in their accelerating improvability. This effort may do, apparently, but little. But mere beginning a good cause is never little. If we can get this vast wheel into any perceptible motion, we shall have accomplished much."

The great challenge that Horace Mann faced was not only to retain the fundamental concept of local control, but also to exert a productive leadership at the State level, a dual mobility that would upgrade the entire system. His success is one of the finest examples in history of what a dedicated man can achieve against overwhelming odds. In the 12 years of his secretaryship, the appropriations for public education more than doubled, salaries for teachers were greatly increased, professional meetings and institutes were conducted throughout the State, a full month was added to the length of the school term, new buildings were erected, sectarian intrusions on State funds were defeated, improved textbooks were adopted, the first three normal schools in America for the training of teachers were founded, innovative teaching techniques from abroad were introduced, and the development of the public high school to replace the private academy was advanced. In addition, as editor of *The Common School Journal*, Mann considered the subject of school hygiene and implemented the concept of school libraries.

Horace Mann must be regarded, therefore, as perhaps the greatest of the "founders" of our American system of free public schools. It was amazing that he accomplished all this in an office that had no authority of command. Yet, his powers of persuasion were such that he fulfilled to the letter his charge from the State:

". . . to collect information of the actual condition and efficiency of the common schools and other means of popular education, and to diffuse as widely as possible, throughout every part of the Commonwealth, information of the most approved and successful methods of arranging the studies, and conducting the education of the young. . . ."

Mann achieved his goals with due respect for a balanced control between the State and local authority. He fully recognized the principle of local autonomy. This was one of the ideals of self-government the Revolution had established. It was not to be bartered away for temporary gain. No one did more than he to establish in the minds of the American people the fundamental principles that education should be universal, nonsectarian, and free, and that its aim should be social efficiency, civic virtue and character building, rather than mere learning or the advancement of sectarian ends. Under his practical leadership an unorganized and heterogeneous series of community school systems were reduced, organized and welded into a unified system. Horace Mann called upon the people of Massachusetts in particular, and Americans in general, to make their support of education for all come alive.

Each of Horace Mann's 12 annual State reports is a landmark in the development of the system. They were, in addition, inspirational examples to educational reformers throughout the Nation. It is, of course, impossible to note the achievements of all the great educators who also con-

Henry Barnard
*Courtesy of the National
Education Association,
Washington, D.C.*

John Swett
*Courtesy of the National
Education Association,
Washington, D.C.*

tributed to improvements similar to those attained under
Horace Mann's leadership in Massachusetts. Yet, brief
mention should be made of Henry Barnard in Connecticut
and Rhode Island, Calvin H. Wiley in North Carolina,
Robert Breckinridge in Kentucky, Caleb Mills in Indiana
and John Swett in California. Each of these men believed
in America and the role of the free public school as a
means of achieving an enlightened citizenry and of preserving our heritage of freedom.

In 1850, the basic concept of a nonsectarian, free, tax-
supported, universal public school system had been firmly
established. It had overcome all attacks. That ideal, under
Horace Mann's guidance, had become a practical reality in
Massachusetts. Other States and other educators followed
this outstanding example. Soon, with the outbreak of the
War Between the States, America's faith in freedom would
again be tested. But the system then had become so much a

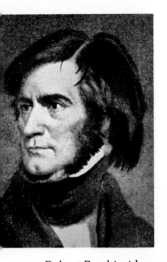

Robert Breckinridge
*Courtesy of the Kentucky
Department of Education.*

Caleb Mills
*Courtesy of the
Indiana State Library,
Indiana Division.*

Calvin H. Wiley
*Courtesy of the North
Carolina State
Department of
Cultural Resources.*

part of our Nation that it would have been unthinkable to return to a fragmented, tuition-supported, church-dominated educational system, so contrary to the New World values of freedom and enlightened living.

After the hiatus of the War Between the States, the history of the American public school was one of adjustment, growth and improvement. The vast majority of the American people were fully in accord with Thaddeus Stevens who, in defending the Free School Law in Pennsylvania, had said:

"If an elective Republic is to endure for any length of time, every elector must have sufficient information not only to accumulate wealth and take care of his pecuniary concerns, but to direct wisely the legislature, the ambassadors, and the Executive of the Nation—for some part of all these things, some agency in approving

45

Thaddeus Stevens
Courtesy of H. Armstrong Roberts, Philadelphia, Pennsylvania.

46

or disapproving of them, falls to every freeman. If, then, the permanency of our Government depends upon such knowledge, it is the duty of Government to see that the means of information be diffused to every citizen. This is a sufficient answer to those who deem education a private and not a public duty."

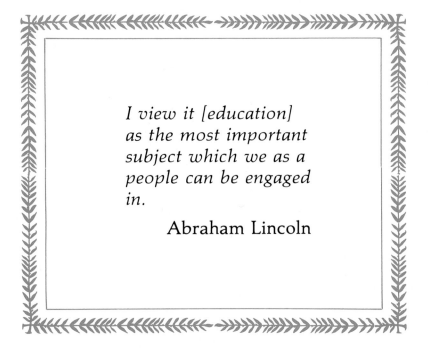

*I view it [education]
as the most important
subject which we as a
people can be engaged
in.*

Abraham Lincoln

THE AMERICAN PUBLIC SCHOOL SYSTEM, 1850-1920:

Seventy Years of Progress

EACH of the two wars—the Revolution and the War Between the States—in turn shook the foundations of public education in America. Wartime trauma, economic upheavals and family disruptions certainly were not conductive to peacetime "reading, writing, and arithmetic."

Once the wars were over, however, on each occasion the people responded with more than adequate repairs. They rebuilt with enthusiasm, realizing the critical importance of maintaining the momentum which the wars had intercepted. It had been demonstrated that the tax-supported public school was the best tool for getting the job done of educating the youth and in a way that strengthened the patriotic ideals and social cohesion, an American melting pot, in the New World setting of human values. If our Republic was to survive and prosper, it would have to be reenforced repetitively with informed leaders and voters. Luckily and wisely, therefore, the disruptions that might have rocked our educational structure off its foundation were repaired. The wounds the wars inflicted were healed.

Great leaders on both sides of the Mason-Dixon Line underlined the need for restoration. For instance, in 1865 the perceptive General Robert E. Lee became president of the present Washington and Lee University in Virginia. He wrote to a friend and described the ruined state of education in the South and asked for immediate action. He said:

"So great have those interests [educational] been disturbed at the South, and so much does its future condition depend upon the rising generation, that I consider the proper education of its youth one of the most important objects now to be attained, and one from which the greatest benefits may be expected. Nothing will compensate us for the depression of the standard of our moral and intellectual culture, and each State should take the most energetic measures to revive the schools and colleges, and, if possible, to increase the facilities for instruction and to elevate the standard of learning."

The General Assembly of the State of Alabama reflected Lee's endeavors in 1867 and moved:

"to enact necessary and proper laws for the encouragement of schools and the means of education."

The Freedmen's Bureau in the South assisted from 1865 to 1870 in this rebuilding effort. This was a well-meant but mismanaged effort of the Federal Government, but over 2,500 schools were established and some 150,000 children were introduced to their first letters. On a higher grade level, General Samuel C. Armstrong of Hampton Institute, Virginia, in 1868, and Booker T. Washington at Tuskegee Institute, Alabama, in 1881, had greater success in bringing education to the newly freed. It became clear, however, that decades of growth and control on the local

Robert E. Le
*Courtesy of the Collection of Washingtc
and Lee University, Lexington, Virgini*

level in the South would be required and without aid or interference from Northern philanthropy in order to rebuild a free public school system. Gradually this was accomplished and in 1900, each of the Southern States compared favorably with any other State in the Union.

Hence, the basic principles of the American free public school system were well-established. Any doubt had been clarified in 1874, when the Supreme Court of the State of Michigan ruled in the case of *Charles E. Stuart et al.* v. *School District No. 1 of the Village of Kalamazoo,* 30 *Michigan,* 69., that taxes to support high schools were permissible under the State constitution of 1850. That decision came 50 years after there was founded in Boston in 1821 the first tax-supported school for students beyond eight years of common schooling. The precedent successfully overcame any later challenges to public school tax levies at any grade level. In fact, all new States, upon admission, enacted laws to support State universities, and these provisions were quickly honored.

The general development from 1850 to World War I, therefore, was not so much a task of innovation as the refinement of an already established and successful system. This adjustment basically realized the ideal that the greatest of American educators, Horace Mann, had in mind when he said on July 4, 1842:

"Remember the child. Pour out light and truth as God pours sunshine and rain. No longer seek knowledge as the luxury of a few, but dispense it amongst all as the bread of life. Summon the mightiest intellects; collect whatever talent or erudition or eloquence or authority the broad land can supply, and Go Forth and Teach this people."

The success of this effort was assured when increased

Harmony School, Stoney Creek Township, Madison County, Indiana
(prior 1900). The community called it the Boot-Jack School.
Courtesy of the National Education Association, Washington, D.C.

School Building in the 60's.
Courtesy of the National Education Association, Washington, D.C.

attention was given to the development of teachers. Under Horace Mann's guidance, Massachusetts was the first State, in 1839, to support a so-called "normal" school for the training of teachers. Practically every State, North and South, later followed this pattern and founded normal schools where the fine art and profession of teaching were taught. This occupation thus was raised from a mere talent or craft easily picked up in haphazard experience.

The teacher in America, unlike her European counterpart, was a woman, especially at the dame school or common levels. When Boston opened its first public high schools for girls in 1826, the advanced education of women had begun. In 1833, Oberlin College became America's first coeducational institution of higher learning. But our first adequately endowed collegiate school for women—Vassar—was not founded until 1861. All State universities beyond the Mississippi, except that of Missouri, admitted women, and the University of Michigan began admitting them in 1870.

The enthusiastic democratization of education taking place throughout the late 19th century in America included the integration of women at all levels of education. The elitist, often religiously oriented academy, for instance, faded away in favor of the public, tax-supported high school which was free of clerical influence and hence responsive to public needs.

America being now fully in the industrial era, it became increasingly clear that students, both male and female, should have practical skills. The result in this direction was threefold: new teaching methods, new subjects and new avenues of instruction.

Until the War Between the States, teaching methods had been traditional. There was what was known as the Lancasterian system, modeled after methods of an English

The common school is the greatest discovery ever made by man. In two grand, characteristic attributes, it is supereminent over all others: first, in its universality—for it is capacious enough to receive and cherish in its parental bosom every child that comes into the world; and second, in the timeliness of the aid it proffers—its early, seasonable supplies of counsel and guidance making security antedate danger. Other social organizations are curative and remedial; this is a preventive and an antidote; they come to heal diseases and wounds; this, to make the physical and moral frame invulnerable to them. Let the common school be expanded to its capabilities, let it be worked with the efficiency of which it is susceptible, and nine-tenths of the crime in the penal code would become obsolete; the long catalog of human ills would be abridged; property, life, and character held by a stronger tenure; all rational hopes respecting the future brightened.

Horace Mann

John Dewey
Courtesy of the National Education Association, Washington, D.C.

schoolmaster, Joseph Lancaster. This stressed rote learning. A teacher or his monitor instructed pupils who then proved their comprehension and memorization through recitation. Basically authoritarian, the method focused attention on the teacher, rather than on the student. The student simply absorbed but never questioned; he was trained, not developed. In contrast, a German-Swiss educator, Johann Pestalozzi, stressed real life "sense impression," not abstract booklearning, and harmonized this experimental data with the natural development of the child. Freedom was stressed and creativity was encouraged. The school was transformed from its traditional role as an instrument of the establishment to a means of developing the free, thinking individual. The German teacher, Friedrich Froebel, a student of Pestalozzi, brought a second European influence to bear on American education. In *The Education of Man* (1826), Froebel stressed preschool development of the student in kindergartens. Here music and creative activities gave the child a positive concept as an individual that would carry through life, making for an eager student and an active mind and citizen. The first American public school kindergarten was started in Massachusetts in 1870, and gradually Froebel's expanded idea of education became part of the American public school system. In fact, recently it has been further enlarged under such programs as "Head Start."

Henry Barnard, the great Connecticut educator, made these ideas of Pestalozzi, Froebel and others available to American teachers from 1855 to 1881, in his *American Journal of Education.* Its 31 volumes were landmarks in American education, and, with the other educational journals that also appeared on the national scene, provided a base for America's most noted modern educational philosopher, John Dewey.

As head of the School of Education at the University of Chicago, John Dewey was the foremost interpreter of the effect on the student of America's social and industrial changes. His basic concept, to use his phrase stated in such books as the *School and Society* in 1899, and *Democracy and Education* in 1916, was that the school was a miniature of "typical conditions of social life." Social efficiency, not mere knowledge, was his goal for education, and he felt this could be best achieved through direct participation in the school as the institution of society. "Learn by doing," became Dewey's motto, and through practical, realistic schoolwork, each student learned how to live amid the complexities of modern social life.

Dewey's approach to the method of education clearly was pragmatic and also determined the content of education. The curriculum evolved in response to the needs of an emerging industrial age. Society could concentrate no longer on only the mental and moral aspects of the student. Although these would remain central to the total student, for success there would be a need of knowledge, of the fundamentals of politics, of economics and of the sciences. As Dewey put it, in "cooperative and mutually useful living." In the traditional curriculum, for instance, history previously had been an informal part of geography and general reading. Now, not only did history become a separate subject, but American history specifically was used to inform the student of our unique national heritage. Other courses related to history—such as political science, civics and contemporary social problems—entered the course of study; thus preparing the student for an active role as a contributing citizen.

Other pragmatic courses, such as physical and health education, became part of the standard curriculum as the year 1880 approached. Similarly, vocational training in

A horsedrawn stagecoach schoolbus, Telluride High School,
district unknown, circa 1910.
Courtesy of the Library of Congress, Washington, D.C.

Modern Schoolbus.

agricultural and mechanic arts, established in the land grant colleges as early as 1862, was introduced into the high school curriculum in 1900. The Smith-Hughes Act of 1917, stimulated even more stress on industrial and commercial courses in high school. While a core curriculum of essential subjects such as English was maintained, students were allowed to elect courses of special academic or vocational interest to them. In addition, intermediate levels of vocationally-oriented evening, junior and community colleges were created so that the student could remain close to home while learning skills that would prepare for service as a beneficial member of the local community. Here it was that the ultimate bloom of the American public school system flourished in local control and support. The school in the first decades of the 20th century had become fully responsive to the people themselves. Boys and girls were admitted to every level from kindergarten to college. The subjects taught were directly related to the full and individual development of each child's total human potential. Governor Brantley Aycock of North Carolina, a great friend of the public schools, reflected this ideal in words cast in bronze on the base of his memorial statue in the United State Capitol. He said:

"Equal! that is the word! On that word I plant myself and my party—the equal right of every child born on earth to have the opportunity to burgeon out all there is within him."

The next development was how these new methods and subjects could reach every American. New avenues of instruction had to be introduced. Until 1852, student attendance was not compulsory. Massachusetts passed the first law to that effect in 1852. This innovation was followed to some degree in nearly every other State, so that in 1900 students were compelled to attend school for at least 20 weeks per year. This limit is now extended to the full school year of each locale. The minimum age now for legally leaving school has risen from 10, to 12, 14, 16 years of age, and often 18 years. This legislation has placed significant new responsibilities upon the American public school system. Aside from educating the willing and able, the school system now must teach the truant, the incorrigible and the delinquent; also the children of the foreign-born who have no English language aptitude, the mentally retarded, the physically handicapped, and those with language disabilities such as the aphasic and dyslexic child. The task is therefore great. The public school system must try to salvage and return to society these special children for socially and personally useful roles.

Though this responsibility is great, it is typically American and is epitomized in our national motto, "Out of Many, One." Out of these many students of differing abilities, regions and backgrounds, the American public school system primarily must create one thing—an American enlightened citizen. The child should know its Nation, have a sense of abiding patriotism, and be willing to contribute a full share to the common good. From this rich diversity there comes unity of purpose and effort.

The period from the War Between the States to World War I—70 years—saw the progress and development of our American public school refined into the successful pattern of public education that great educators as Horace Mann and John Dewey had envisioned. Teaching methods were improved, and the student was taught both the value of his special individual character and the ability to think for himself. The curriculum emerged into a viable response to the changing needs of an industrial, democratic society. School attendance was made compulsory so

James Bryant Conant
Courtesy of National Education Association, Washington, D.C.

that each child of whatever inclination or ability could be assured an education.

In 1945, James Bryant Conant, president of Harvard University, said in his seminal book, *General Education in a Free Society*, that:

"Our purpose is to cultivate in the largest possible number of our future citizens an appreciation of both the responsibilities and the benefits which come to them because they are Americans and are free."

As America entered World War I, an opportunity was presented to test the results of the educational foundation upon which our society was erected. A challenge to our system thereby took on worldwide proportions. Our fighting forces marched under the banner of human rights as derived from the freedoms we had been taught and enjoyed on our own shores. We were forced to grapple with an enemy that did not share those ideals. It became our mission to prove the validity and strength of human values, respect for the individual, and our faith in freedom.

The laudable humanitarian target of this vital center of American life, from which the vast majority of our Armed Forces came, reflected the wisdom of the Republic in teaching children how to make a living and how to live a life. Patriotism had been inculcated in a country which nurtured pride in a heritage of freedom, much as an Athenian youth responded with a vow that many of us learned in school. Consequently, when our men and women returned to the United States, their training had been tested in the fiery furnace of international conflict, and while "making the world safe for democracy" now may appear elusive, they knew that in their homeland there was a place where the winds of freedom blew over a victorious Republic.

What our schools do may prove in the long run to be more decisive than any other factor in preserving the form of government we cherish.

Franklin Delano Roosevelt

THE AMERICAN
PUBLIC SCHOOL SYSTEM:

The Last Fifty Years

As America emerged from the travail of World War I, the public school outlook was bleak. It had hit a bottom low. I recall on a trip to Chicago hearing groups of teachers shouting: "We want our pay!" Their checks had been held back for lack of funds. Before that, in California, about 1919, the schools were short 1,200 teachers. Some 600 schools had been closed. Overlarge classes contained an average of 80 pupils. Many teachers lacked special training and preparations. These conditions required immediate and effective action. There was a crying need that the parents and the public be aware of the disastrous consequences of continued apathy and neglect.

Then it was that a most dramatic and dynamic event occurred. There arose upon the scene in San Francisco an attorney and Thirty-third Degree Mason, the then Grand Master of Masons, Charles Albert Adams. Over vigorous objections of his peers who thought this was the type of political problem that regular Masonry should eschew, he persuaded the Grand Lodge to proclaim the week commencing September 27, 1920, Public Schools Week, and to initiate a program to alert all segments of the Californian citizenry of the needs and steps required for corrections. He pointed out that as President McKinley said, "Our agreements are principles; our differences are politics." Also, he underlined that there was a difference between political science and partisan politics.

As a result, committees were appointed in the Masonic Lodges throughout the State. They made appraisals and inspections of public school activities and needs. The people were informed and galvanized into intense concern and action. The enthusiasm was contagious and generated long-delayed improvements and reforms. Constitutional provisions were enacted that assured sufficient and secure funding. Allocations were measured upon pupil attendance.

Surprising benefits resulted from that beginning. The movement spread to other States and activated similar annual observances throughout the Nation. These included not only Masonic organizations but others also interested in public schools. Programs and inspections of the schools were organized in all localities with the assistance of school administrative staffs. Qualified speakers told of conditions affecting public education. Thus, the wholesome results of an alert interest were brought home to the parents and the public.

Each succeeding Grand Master of Masons in California and those in many other States issued proclamations for similar annual observances. These, combined with those of related organizations which patterned programs upon the California forerunner, continued with slogans and opportunities for community participation and visits and public relations outlets. Sponsorship did not necessarily

Charles Albert Adams

Early Classroom
*Courtesy of the
Library of
Congress,
Washington, D.C.*

**Modern
Classroom**
*Courtesy of the
National Education
Association,
Washington, D.C.*

imply endorsement of the actions and programs of the schools. How well they performed could best be judged through the results. Student performance in California, for example, where Public Schools Week has been held annually now for 59 years, ranked among the highest in the Nation.

Thus, in addition to the needs and improvements required, there was a reminder of the public school purpose, and an image created of friendship, faith and confidence. The public school motivators did this, not as political agitators nor as contentious critics, but as intelligent periodic appraisers of what the schools were doing and how they could do better. The activities were political only in the sense that the organizations were deeply concerned with active and important civic affairs, and were patriotic participants in modern avenues of effective good citizenship, with a feeling of pride and gratitude that here in the United States we had and should maintain the finest system of public education in the world.

The intervening World Wars I and II put public school officials under severe pressure to produce students primarily adept at technology. Other goals were also diverted. But the American system has remained true to producing above all, an enlightened, cohesive and freedom-loving citizenry. This mission was clearly stated in a 1943 report of President James Bryant Conant to the Board of Overseers, Harvard University. Dr. Conant observed:

"The primary concern of American education today is not the development of the appreciation of the 'good life' in young gentlemen born to the purple . . . . Our purpose is to cultivate in the largest possible number of our future citizens an appreciation of both the responsibilities and benefits which come to them because they are Americans and are free."

As a national report on American universal education stated in 1958:

"Not only must we have competent people in a wide range of key professions, but underlying it also have an informed citizenry. Among the tasks that have increased most frighteningly in complexity, is the task of the ordinary citizen who wishes to discharge his civic responsibilities intelligently."

To accomplish the public school goal of an informed and enlightened citizenry, an expanded program had been developed in the 1930's which pursued two apparently contradictory but truly complementary objectives—generalization and specialization. This twofold character was evident in the leadership of such educators as Robert M. Hutchins, president of the University of Chicago. He proposed the introduction in intermediate or junior high school, and even in college curricula, of "fusion courses." American history and literature, for instance, were combined, or economics, sociology and civics merged, to become a course in "Problems of Democracy."

The idea of treating the "total personality" of the student was extended to the rapid increase of "extracurricular" activities such as music, chorus, theatre, radio, biology, geology and astronomy clubs or groups. Many of these extracurricular functions allowed the student to follow broad fields that satisfied personal interests, thus enriching the total personality. Health, athletic and sports activities were also expanded. Professionals trained in physical education became part of the standard curriculum for both boys and girls. The ancient Greek ideal of a

Because our schools help shape the mind and character of our youth, the strength or weakness of our educational system today will go far to determine the strength or weakness of our national wisdom and our national morality tomorrow. That is why it is essential to our nation that we have good schools. And their quality depends on all of us.

Dwight D. Eisenhower

sound mind in a sound body became a reality in American education.

This theme of general education was complemented with a clear-eyed and realistic awareness that specialization was a fact of modern life. In addition, the hardships of the Great Depression of the 1930's made it evident that technical skills were necessary for economic survival. The expenditures for our public schools doubled every decade from 1880 to 1930, thus vindicating our American faith in universal education. In the 1930's this was increased even more with grants and subsidies from the Federal Government. As part of the "New Deal" and, later, the "Fair Deal," American public education was assisted at every level of local, state and national government. It was big business. For instance, in 1965, over $42 billion in tax revenue was spent on public schools to educate 54 million students up to the age of 17 who were attending 125,000 schools, staffed with 100,000 administrators and 2 million teachers. The American public school system, aside from being a development laboratory and generator of a free society, clearly is a gigantic industry and touches every aspect of our intellectual, economic and social life.

These figures indicate clearly that contrary to the situation of World War I, the stringent years of World War II did not affect public support of the school system. The Armed Forces, it is true, stripped classrooms of young male teachers but concerned individuals joined the National Education Association, the National Citizens' Commission for Public Schools, the National Teachers' Association, the Parent-Teacher Association and other groups that helped assure a public school system responsive to the needs of society and of the student. Washington, also, continued its concern and assistance. Whereas the Smith-Hughes Act of 1917 had provided Federal aid to secondary schools offering agricultural and mechanical education, the George-Deen Act, amended as the George-Borden Act of 1946, encouraged the inclusion of business and commercial aspects into the expanding public school studies. A post-World War II boom of students were brought into the college level of American public education. The $14.5 billion invested in GI benefits clearly revealed America's commitment to education of the citizen-soldier.

It perhaps should be observed in passing at this point that our United States Supreme Court has applied the American doctrine of church-state separation solidly with respect to elementary and secondary church schools. The State cannot furnish aid in any form to such under-collegiate church schools. There has been some relief afforded, however, to collegiate church schools. While proponents of State aid to church-schools are currently agitating for tuition grants or credits or vouchers to parents whose children attend elementary or secondary church schools, these plans are opposed as violating the First Amendment to the United States Constitution. But, even the proponents now have awakened to possible boomerangs and traps. For, as has been held with references to church schools of collegiate level, the granting of governmental aid even to only one attending student makes the schools recipient institutions and, hence, results in full Federal control. This could be a fate worse than death! A horde of bureaucratic ferrets would be unleashed under a variety and complexity of myriads of regulations. These would include those of the Civil Rights Act of 1964, and would require interminable reports on pupils, faculty, administrative staff, specifying sex, race and ethnic background. The paperwork alone would inundate any institution. The Federal bureaucracy would call

73

the shots on all programs and activities, including in the case of religious related schools, the removal of crosses and other symbols and church indicia. It is questionable whether such a school could retain its Christian or Judaic character. The cost of compliance and in filling out Federal forms would be staggering. More important than this, however, would be the alien bureaucratic intrusion into teaching, research and studies. The boomerangs and traps, therefore, would bring swirling streams of red tape and eventual strangulation.

The "Cold War" of the 1950's supported the "generalist" aspect of the public school system in that courses in history, literature, sociology, economics and the arts demonstrated America's unique heritage of freedom. A student with this background learned what it meant to be an American. He realized liberty was essential for the full development of every individual. Armed with a diploma from the American public school, he was fortified against political and kindred forms of attempted tyranny or despotism.

In 1957, the "Cold War" also brought the shock of "Sputnik", Soviet Russia's first space satellite. As a Nation we suddenly found ourselves technologically in second place. There was a renewed stress then on practical specialization. The National Defense Education Act of 1958 encouraged instruction in mathematics, the sciences and foreign languages. This endeavor succeeded in upgrading the overall and scientific quality of American education. One result was apparent when America's astronaut, Neil Armstrong, placed an American flag on the Moon, and said, "That's one small step for man, one giant leap for mankind."

The American public school system has continued its twofold program of developing both the generalist and the specialist. The consolidation of smaller schools into larger, better equipped regional or district schools has broadened the base of the expanded curriculum. In addition, these schools have adopted increased health programs. Similarly, the classroom environment has benefited from consolidations because both teachers and students can use the latest in audiovisual equipment such as slides, films and videotapes. Professionally trained teachers, guidance counselors, educational psychologists, speech therapists, administrators and many other specialists have provided a coherent and coordinated environment which is more capable of meeting the needs of every pupil for entry into the modern competitive world.

A long distance had elapsed from the first tentative moves in 17th century New England toward tax-supported general education. Many problems have been overcome. America has created a free, universal public school system that has served our country well and is the envy of many others. It has provided a base for understanding our cultural heritage. The emphasis on patriotism and freedom has inbued generations of youth with beneficial virtues and ideals of liberty. Our American Way of Life has been preserved through our Nation's two centuries of often turbulent history, largely with the help of the American public school system. Support for this has been won on a basis of merit and as an essential ingredient of our future greatness. Otherwise, that precious birthright easily might have been lost.

The system, undoubtedly, has its faults. Critiques show there have been disappointments to people in some communities. These complaints include crime and immorality, erosion of purpose, classroom misbehavior, inferior performance, failure to instill patriotic values, teachers with an eye on a paycheck rather than on a vision of the child's

Character education takes place every hour of the school day. It takes place when five-year-olds learn to take turns with the new toy rather than to fight for it; in the opening exercises of the country school as the children are asked by their teacher to explain the meaning of ". . . with liberty and justice for all"; on the playground when the "gang" tells the trouble-maker to play by the rules or get out;

. . . in the eighth-grade history class which makes posters to illustrate the immortal ideals of the American Declaration of Independence—"all men are created equal . . . endowed by their Creator with certain unalienable rights . . . life, liberty, and the pursuit of happiness";

. . . in the high school homeroom as the students decide what message to send to the girl who has been stricken with polio;

. . . in the English class that studies Macbeth or the Vision of Sir Launfal;

. . . on the class picnic, on the football field, in the rehearsal for the senior play, in the social-service project of the sociology class, in the community beautification project of the civics class;

. . . in the developing insights into the nature of truth in the geometry class and the physics laboratory;

. . . when a disturbed adolescent shares his troubles with a trusted counselor . . . when youth observe exemplary character in their teachers.

Dr. Willard E. Givens

life and place in society. Yet, these deficiencies are exposed only in a free society such as ours, and they are few indeed when compared to the magnificent and overall accomplishments. Moreover, many times the protests come from isolated but more publicized areas.

We still struggle for improvements, to expand the wholesome scope, to make more relevant an application to every student, to maintain discipline and order, to assist the potential "dropout" and to reach the recent immigrant. When occasional grumblers sound off, an irrefutable answer is available. For, the improvement sought or the complaint made puts the focus where it primarily belongs: on participation of local concerned citizens. There lies the remedial key.

The more we know and value the unique American system, the more effectively we can resolve and correct the flaws and bestow credit where it is due. Thereby we form and hold together our Nation as an educational fortress against the intrusion of alien, wornout concepts that we have long since discarded. Hopefully, what we have achieved may serve as a pattern for expansion elsewhere in the world. And so, as we support the American public school system, we, too, become national and universal builders of freedom, part of a glorious past, a great present and even greater future. Let us always remember the inspiring words of Daniel Webster: "God grants liberty only to those who love it, and are always ready to guard and defend it." So, also, with freedom's cornerstone: the American public school system.

Early Instruction
*Courtesy of the Library of
Congress, Washington, D.C.*

Modern Instruction
Courtesy of the National Education Association, Washington, D.C.

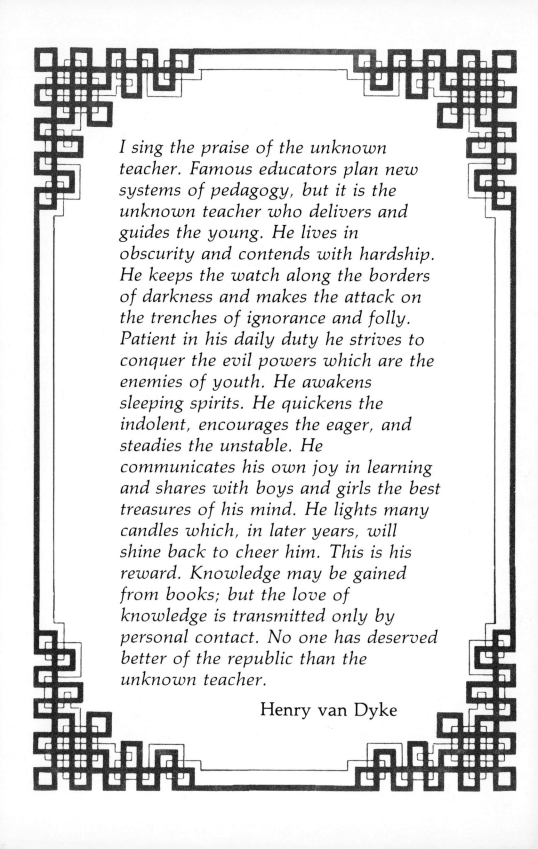

I sing the praise of the unknown teacher. Famous educators plan new systems of pedagogy, but it is the unknown teacher who delivers and guides the young. He lives in obscurity and contends with hardship. He keeps the watch along the borders of darkness and makes the attack on the trenches of ignorance and folly. Patient in his daily duty he strives to conquer the evil powers which are the enemies of youth. He awakens sleeping spirits. He quickens the indolent, encourages the eager, and steadies the unstable. He communicates his own joy in learning and shares with boys and girls the best treasures of his mind. He lights many candles which, in later years, will shine back to cheer him. This is his reward. Knowledge may be gained from books; but the love of knowledge is transmitted only by personal contact. No one has deserved better of the republic than the unknown teacher.

Henry van Dyke